Understanding
Effective Use of Statistics
Checklist & Guide

Understanding and Making Effective Use of Statistics

Checklist & Guide

Leonard Seymour-Smith

Management Update

First published in Great Britain 1985 by
Management Update Ltd, 43 Brodrick Road,
London SW17 7DX

British Library Cataloguing in Publication
Data:
Seymour-Smith, Leonard
Understanding and making effective use of
statistics: guide & checklist
1. Business mathematics   2. Mathematical
statistics
I. Title
519.5'024658 HF5691

ISBN 0 946679 11 8 (Paperback)
ISBN 0 946679 12 6 (Hardback)

Illustrations by Timothy Nevil

Typeset by Budget Typesetting (London) Ltd
Printed in Great Britain by Anchor Brendon Ltd,
Tiptree, Essex

Contents

The author, Leonard Seymour-Smith B. Com (Dunelm), MIS, MBIM, FSS runs a successful consultancy service both for public and private sector organisations. He has considerable experience of lecturing, running management training seminars and undertaking research projects.

After studying at the universities of Goettingen and Durham he graduated in managerial economics and statistics. He was an economic advisor, HM Treasury until taking up a post as Team Leader in Economics and Business studies at the City of Westminster College. Later he joined management consultants Inbucon International as a senior consultant in their marketing and business planning division.

He has contributed many articles to professional journals and is author of a number of books including 'The Business Environment' and 'Planning for business and Social Responsibility': he has also written numerous successful study manuals for colleges and tuition centres.

Preface

Handling and understanding statistics is a basic requirement in business, public administration and many other walks of life yet there is a widespread tendency to shy away from anything statistical. No doubt the unfamiliar technology and jargon don't help but the main stumbling block is often a fear of the mathematical concepts and formulae involved.

This book aims to provide concise and practical guidelines to enable the reader to grasp basic statistical concepts and dispel some of the fears and myths which so often surround the subject.

With the aid of numerous examples I have tried to help the reader not only to understand how best to present and examine data, but to analyse and interpret it and set about making forecasts. I have deliberately tried to keep the text simple and restrict myself to those statistical ideas which are of practical value — particularly to the business executive — and avoided any areas which involve more than a knowledge of very elementary mathematics. It may come as a surprise to find that a great deal can be achieved statistically speaking without recourse to higher mathematics and formulae which leave the layman cold!

1. Introduction

Now have you ever been faced with having to:
- find something (but WHAT?) to say about the mass of figures which have been passed over to you?
- discover some way of reducing the enormous tables of figures to a mere handful of meaningful — and actually understandable — statistics?
- make other people interested in YOUR facts at a time when they are generally beset by such a large amount of statistical information released (or thrust upon them) by Governments Departments, Local Authorities, pressure groups and other organisations of all shapes and sizes and authority?
- discern patterns, trends, cycles, and make a basic forecast without having to rely upon the help of experts?

You have? What exactly did you do to solve your problem?

Do you still believe that you have to have a first-class honours degree in mathematics before you can handle statistics meaningfully?

Yes? Then, you're quite wrong, as this book intends to show you.

WHAT IS, OR ARE, STATISTICS?

Statistics *is* a collection of methods and processes which have the objective of collecting, analysing and making conclusions about meaningful numbers.

Statistics *are* meaningful numbers such as the monthly salary you receive, the price of the car you couldn't buy, or the mileage claim you made last week, Since we can't organise society, or a firm, on the basis of trial and error, or guesswork, these statistics are the foundation of very many national and organisational decisions. If we want to 'go over the top' about them, we could claim that they are a major factor in human progress!

STATISTICAL LIES?

Let's get one thing straight. Yes, you can prove anything with statistics. Provided, that is, you miss out the data you don't like, slip in figures you do like, or otherwise maneouvre the statistics so that the wrong story is told. The figures themselves, when correct, don't lie, or mislead. It's people who do that!

Statistics have to have both a purpose and a meaning. They relate, that is, to facts, and they can only cope with things which are countable or measurable. Yet, a statistical fact isn't of any use or interest to you unless it is somehow able to be linked with other facts. If a factory production line has a 'reject-rate' of 1 in 1,000, we may think this is good or bad, but it's only until we realise that last quarter the rate was 100 in 1,000 that we can form a real opinion!

Our statistics aren't any use in isolation, then. Their use lies in the comparisons they offer us. So we may have, say, a comparison of:

- actual figures for one location with actual figures for other locations (e.g. sales of different branches of the same group; or
- actual figures for a given period of time with similar figures for other periods (e.g. sales of Product X last year with those of the previous year); or
- figures put as percentages of some common element either in time or at a location (e.g. the number of bicycles per 1,000 of the population in Western Germany and the UK).

So, what can we say are the objectives of using statistics, then? Three objectives, really, and these are:

- PRESENTING PAST FACTS, changes being clearly revealed through analysis and comparison, and looking at those facts in relation to the most recent figures available.
- PROVISION OF UP-TO-DATE data for comparison with past data, so that we can find out alternatives and trends.
  THE FORECASTING of future conditions with reasonable probability they will arise (so that we can make plans).

PRIMARY AND SECONDARY STATISTICS

It is useful for you to understand that there are two basic kinds of figures available to us:

> **primary statistics**, which are collected at first hand by various means, for a special purpose, and are as yet lying in a large and untreated mass; and

> **secondary statistics**, which are 'treated' (processed) and already otherwise handled.

Of course, your secondary data can become someone else's primary data.

Why bother to make the distinction? Only because if you are presented with secondary data, then you have to make sure how careful the compilers have been, what *their* sources were and what the degree of accuracy aimed at — and attained — was. Remember that 'Somebody else's statistics' can be full of traps and stumbling blocks. But more about that later on.

CAUTION

On the threshold of discovering the 'secrets' of understanding and making effective use of your statistics, you have to understand that statistical methods and techniques (every highly sophisticated one requiring a computer!)

don't automatically bestow upon you a kind of magic omnipotency. The successful manager, with his years of experience, is probably able to forecast, say, sales far better for next year than a Business School whizz-kid with a doctorate in mathematical statistics who knows nothing about the business!

But, an awareness of the kind of thing we are discussing in this booklet WILL provide you with a knowledge of the many and various flaws possessed by existing sources of statistics and techniques. This awareness obviously protects you from the very common misuses of statistical materials and lets you gain as much advantage as you can from applying the proper methods in handling figures.

STATISTICAL COUNTING AND MEASUREMENT

Statistics concerns both counting and measurement, We can, for instance, *count* separate objects or individuals (which are separated by some distinctive marking or other, like 'brunette' or 'blonde') but we have to measure others using special units.

For example, people, cars, cats, buildings, flying saucers can be counted. On the other hand, coal, water, income, and road mileage have to be measured.

Some things can be counted *or* measured; money, for example, or shipping.

The point is that some of the 'units of measurement' we use are taken from technical areas, some are borrowed from everyday speech and yet others are created specially for the job. This means you must be very careful indeed about getting the right 'specification' because statistics require more careful handling than your everyday conversation does!

To emphasise what we mean, here are four major rules about using units for measurement:

1. The unit simply has to be very specific and clear
You have to have:
- note of any special meanings,
- no ambiguity at all,
- special rules for marginal cases, and
- arbitrary characteristics if needbe.

Take the term ACCIDENT. What IS it, exactly? An 'accident' could be
> any injury, no matter how trivial it is,
> one requiring some medical attendance,
> one which is *reported* officially,
> one causing absence from work, or
> one for which compensation is liable.

What does it matter? Well, if you are in insurance your concern will tend to lie in the last two types. The Health and safety expert will be interested in the reported cases.

2. The unit has to be stable
Currency in general isn't. The rate of exchange varies, for example, and so does purchasing power.

3. The unit has to be uniform and it has to be homogeneous
The unit musn't signify different things at different times. 'Year' could mean tax year or it could mean calendar year.

4. The unit must be appropriate
The term 'population' may, or may not, be appropriate. It will depend upon whether we mean people permanently resident (minus those away at present?) or whatever.

Of course, we sometimes develop composite units. We may measure railway movements in terms of 'passenger ton miles', or work in 'foot-pounds'.

DO TAKE CARE WITH NUMBERS!

Actually, if you think about it, we can put business information out in three ways:
- in words
- in picture language (e.g. piecharts, graphs), or
- in figures.

Yes, we have to take care in communicating facts using words, written or spoken, but in using figures even greater care is required of us. Make an error in using words and often the result is rubbish and the error is seen clearly for what it is. Make an error using figures and the error is often not seen at all.

Take the statement:
    'The car is in the dog, so he's safe.'
This is rubbish.......unless the car was an edible toy......and this is seen immediately. You can assume this and change the word order.

However, suppose I quote:
    'The car registration number was A754JUG.'
How (unless you had prior information) could you tell that this is wrong? Actually, the number was A574JUG.

SIGNIFICANT STATISTICS

Of course, each figure used in a specific number has a meaning. But it might well be easier on the eye (and the memory!) if you are able to ease the burden a bit.

Suppose the journey from your home to your office happens to be 6 miles, 753 yards, 5 inches? Would it really matter if you claimed it was 'just over 6 miles'? Make no mistake here. The full distance is correct. It is only that such detail really isn't necessary. In fact, it would sound odd if you went around giving the full (and correct) distance.

This leads us to the importance of *'approximation'* in statistics. Suppose you have been given the number

506,743

'Rounded' to the nearest thousand this would be 507,000. Since 743 is clearly in excess of 500. We round up if we see that the digit after the one in the last required 'column' is 5 or over. We round down if it is less than 5. The main issue here is: do be consistent!

In our example above, we refer to the statistic quoted as 'correct to two significant figures' by the way. For example, the sun is (to two significant figures) 93,000,000 miles from the earth. In statistics we really don't have the objective of getting figures correct to the last digit, but we only want to use figures *correct to the extent of accuracy needed for the task we are doing.*

This question of the degree of accuracy required is important. Take population statistics. The total for the UK in 1983 is officially given as 56 millions. That of France as 54.0 million. It's much easier to compare these two populations than the (allegedly) complete figures of 56, 465,518 and 54,003,987. Actually, the two 'actual' populations are faked by the author. But who can prove it? A figure of 50-odd millions can't be checked, anyway. And does it really matter?

To the professional statistician, in any case, figures are usually only estimates because it is usually quite impossible and/or unnecessary to calculate correct to the last digit.

DOES IT MATTER HOW APPROXIMATE THE APPROXIMATION IS?

Well, see for yourself. Take the following figures (tons sold);

Sales (tons)	Sales (tons) (to nearest thousand)	ERROR
79,642	80	+358
5,746	6	+254
13,303	13	−303
15,600	16	+400
14,201	14	−201
29,306	29	−306
503	1	+497
7,790	8	+210
166,091	167	+909

So, we can see that the error (called 'unbiassed') is +909.

If we put it as a percentage it is: 0.544311377% (sorry! we mean 0.544%, or even 0.54%!). What has happened is that the plus and minus figures offset each other to some extent — which is why the overall error is 'unbiassed'.

But what difference would it make if we have simply 'rounded up' always and 'rounded down' always? Look again:

We could approximate to the nearest thousand *above*

80	
6	
14	
16	The error (biassed) is thus
15	+3909, or +2.30%
30	(actually, it's +2.299%).
1	
8	
170	

or we could approximate to the nearest thousand *below*

79	
5	
13	This error (biassed) is thus
15	−4091, or −2.53%
14	(actually, it's −2.525%).
29	
0	
7	
162	

Obviously, if we have to have 'errors' and 'approximations' (and we do) then we'd settle everytime for the unbiassed kind.

Can we, then, banish biassed errors from our business activities? No! If we carry out a survey SOME people (sexist chauvinist pigs, probably) claim that women will tend to understate their age if they're over forty. That'll produce a bias alright!

One final thing. If you look at our first set of figures, you'll see again that we said the error was '+909'. That conveys very little to us if we can't recall the actual size of the total figures in the first place. For this reason we call this statement the 'absolute error'. For all practical purposes it's the percentage (or 'relative') error which is more revealing.

2. Presenting Statistics

INTRODUCING THE IDEA

You can't just simply 'present' statistics. There are a few questions you have to ask about it first of all:

1. *Why* do you have to present them, anyway? Routine? Special event, report?

2. *Who* will be looking at them? Specialists? Or people who know nothing about the subject to which the statistics will relate? People who have to be *made* to be interested?

3. Do you have to present a report, with statistics, *orally*? If so, you will almost certainly need some sort of handout or basic visual aid.

4. From *where* will you be getting your statistics?
    Will they be handed to you, on a plate?
    Will you have to look them up in books, journals, official collections, internal records?
    Will you have to collect them by survey?

5. Will you bear in mind, always, that statistics you present represent facts, and that you can't do things with those figures which you couldn't do with those facts?

'So you are going to present some figures?'

6.	Will you also remember that your statistics are only really basic 'commonsense' plus a little arithmetic?

7.	How are you going to present them, then? What is the 'best' way on this particular occasion?

TRY TABULATING?

Can it be that the old, familiar statistical table will be the order of the day? Well, first of all, let's just look at the kind of things which figures in the original form in which we get them can show:

(i)	they may measure the *change in quantity over a period of time* (i.e. they are 'time series', or 'chronological' data);

(ii)	they may measure the *change in quantity over a geographical area* ('geographical' data);

(iii)	they may show the *presence, or the absence, of a specific characteristic* (e.g. the number of Irish Wolfhounds present at a dog show); or,

(iv)	they may show the *actual size of some characteristic* or other, of something (e.g. weight, in tonnes).

DO YOU THINK THIS IS A GOOD TABLE?

Table A   LSS Plc Product sales (£)

	1960	1970	1980
Total sales	1,176,301	1,179,400	1,183,333
Model I	83,740	106,302	100,942
Model II	10,600	5,064	22,701
Model III	1,081,961	1,068,034	1,059,690
Distribution			
Direct sales	89,060	102,807	261,703
Wholesalers	740,941	774,594	727,553
Retailers.	346,300	301,999	194,077

Source: Wotonerth, 1984

In fact, at first sight, it doesn't seem too bad, does it? Columns and rows, not too many, clearly set out.

But look at the *figures themselves*. Ask yourself:
● How do I summarise these?
● Could I tell a colleague about them on the telephone?
● Could I actually present them orally at a meeting?
● How long would I have to study this table in order to remember the salient points?
● Come to think of it, what **are** the salient points?

LET'S SEE IF WE CAN PRODUCE A BETTER TABLE, THEN

Table B   LSS Plc Product sales (£'000)

	1960	1970	1980
Model I	84	106	101
Model II	11	5	23
Model III	1,082	1,068	1,060
Total sales	1,176	1,179	1,183
By direct sales	89	103	262
By wholesalers	741	775	728
By retailers	346	302	194
Total sales	1,176	1,179	1,183

You can now see the 'pattern' more clearly. What **is** the pattern? Well:

Total sales are rising, but extremely slowly, but the behaviour of individual Model sales is erratic, and sales of Model III appear to falling.

As far as channels are concerned, sales on a direct basis are rising very sharply, whereas sales by wholesalers are behaving erratically. On the other hand, sales by retailers are falling sharply.

But about the lower half of the table. Could this be improved by either inserting, or by substituting, percentage shares? It does depend upon what you want to show, doesn't it? You could produce your table so that it looked like this:

Table C   LSS Plc Sales by Product and Channels of distribution

Sales by Product: £000's	1960	1970	1980
Model I	84	106	101
Model II	11	5	23
Model II	1,082	1,068	1,060
Total	1,176	1,179	1,183

Percentage of total sales through channels of distribution

	1960 %	1970 %	1980 %
Direct sales	7.6	8.7	22.1
Wholesale	63.0	65.7	61.5
Retail	29.4	25.6	16.4
	100.0	100.0	100.0

Simpler? Always look at the possibility of simplifying your tables. Oh, and when you do establish percentages, **do** make sure they actually add up to 100%, and not 99.8% or 101%! Even if you have to make very minor arbitrary adjustments so that they do!

Of course, the design and content of your table will always have to relate in some way to its objective. Yet, irrespective of that, Table B is easier to use than Table A anyway. So, broadly speaking is Table C, too.

The bigger the mass of figures we have to look at (especially if our desk in-tray is usually overloaded), the more highly appreciative we are of simplification. So, let's look at some ground rules which are aimed at helping us to produce good (i.e. effective) tables which do hand people a message or two.

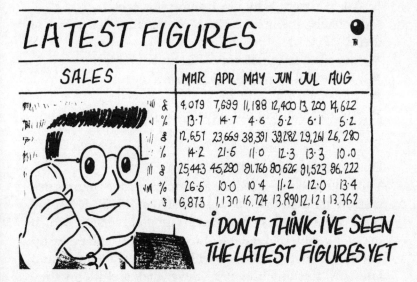

'Large tables do tend to get ignored'

Checklist for Tables

In drawing up your table you have to use imagination, tempered with a little commonsense. There's nothing even vaguely 'mathematical' about this approach! It isn't sufficient to have row after row of figures in columns. The following checklist will help you to produce sound tables:

1. Ask yourself: why am I doing this table?
Most likely the reason is a combination of some of these:
- to show original figures in an *orderly way*;
- to reveal some *distinct pattern*;
- to *summarise*; and/or
- to *record* important figures for others to use as and when necessary.

How simple can I make it?
You have a choice: produce a complex mass of figures in a massive table so that people will sigh and look at it some other time, or design a much simpler version which everyone can understand. Some people will draw up highly complicated tables with dozens of columns and lines, just to show how very clever they are! If only they knew! It's much more clever to introduce people to a

plain, unvarnished and simple table they actually comprehend.

Remember that several simple ones are usually much better than one big, complex one.

3. How shall I describe the contents in a title?

A title is essential, of course. A long-winded one is a pain and can mislead. We could have entitled our previous tables in this way:

> 'Table of the sales of three products (Model I, Model II, Model III) of LSS Plc, in pounds sterling, and sales obtained through various channels of distribution (direct sales, wholesale sales and retail sales), for the three years 1960, 1970 and 1980).'

But what would have been the point of that? If we really had to use a lengthy title we could simply condense it into a main (block capital) title and then amplify it as a subtitle.

Your title should, of course, be comprehensive and explanatory, but no longer than necessary.

4. How shall I state the units clearly?

This is important. There are various conventions, but as a rule this kind of indication is adopted:

> £000's or, sometimes £K; £billion; m working days lost; % of sales; '000 gross tonnes; % per year.

(* however, if you are mature in years you will have been taught that a billion is 1,000,000,000,000; however, that *was* the British billion, and today we have the US billion in tow i.e. 1,000,000,000!).

5. What about row and column headings?
You must not pernit any doubts to creep into your statistics-user's mind. No ambiguity, and, if necessary, add a footnote.

6. How shall I show totals?

Should I show them as follows?		or like this?
8	8	
9	9	
6	6	
23		23
3	3	
4	4	
2	2	
9		9
32	32	

The first method could be confusing (to the hard-pressed, busy user); the second is perfectly clear.

Any awkward and big total should always be suitably broken-up into smaller sections, where this can be done, and the totals collected together in a summary form (as in the adjacent column in the second example above.

7. In what way can I help the table-user to make comparisons?
Well, comparison and calculation will be helped a good

deal where numbers in the same column are so laid out that the decimal place and figures to the left and right of it in any row lie in vertical line with the decimal place and the corresponding figures in any other row.

And, if there is a comparison to be made, then the two sets of figures to be compared ought to be put in parallel columns — where this can be done — next to each other.

8. What else can I do to help the user?
If the figures you are presenting are completely new and original, and if the story they tell is not easy for a particular group of people to work out from statistics alone, then a brief narrative would help. Why not? Provided, that is, you resist the temptation to insert your own *views* rather than *facts*! 'Making' statistics reveal what you want them to say is sometimes a great temptation, but must be resisted.

Remember you can also use different coloured ink, different type faces or sizes and/or differing thicknesses of column rulings to emphasise points.

9, What about the source?
It is important to notify users from whence the statistics came. For one thing, they may want to amplify the information or check up on something. Or, again, they may not remember (neither may you) in twenty years time what the source was!

10. Do I want to include the 'straight' figures, or percentages or ratios — or 'averages'?

If you are providing a simple record, simple figures are usually desirable. If not, do consider percentages (we'll look at averages later on) and ask yourself what they 'give' to the table which it otherwise wouldn't have.

TABLES HELP BECAUSE

- they allow you to locate figures quickly,
- they provide comparisons between different sets of figures,
- they show patterns in the figures which are not seen in, say, narrative form, and
- they do take up less space than other forms of presentation.

JUST TO REMIND YOU

Sort out (classify) your figures, or divide them up into specifically defined groupings so that each group is clearly distinct from the rest. Then draw up your table(s) and set out the figures in the minimum space with the minimum wording.

And don't forget about approximation, because it really can be a help. Absolute precision in business statistics (as opposed to applied science) is not only rare — whatever anyone tries to tell you to the contrary — but usually a waste of time and effort. Sound approximations can be much more cost-effective!

3. If you don't use a table, what alternatives have you?

THE ANSWER IS: DIAGRAMS, CHARTS OR GRAPHS

We don't want to get involved in semantic problems, so let's begin by pointing out that we are going to use the first two of these three terms to mean '*illustrative diagrams*' and the term 'graphs' to mean '*analytical diagrams*'.

SO, WHAT ABOUT ILLUSTRATIVE DIAGRAMS?

These are supposed to
● catch the eye
● give information
The art is that of conveying information to anyone, even those who don't know much about the topic anyway. So they don't need to be accompanied by a table , do they, if that's what they do?

We'll take a look at a few of these now.

1. Pictures (pictograms, isotypes, picturegrams)

This is the easiest and clearest way of producing information about plain figures. The'picture' is obviously connected with the subject. So we might have:

LSS Company, Plc: Progress in house-building (hundreds of units)

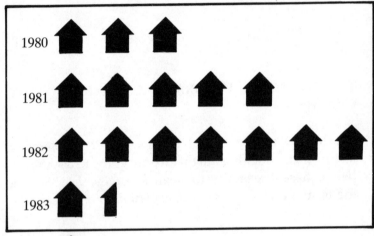

KEY ![house] = 100 units completed

Of course, we have a problem in working out how many the last 'house' represents: 50, perhaps? why not 51? or 48? who knows? Does it matter much?

Accuracy isn't the strong point of this form of statistical presentation, but, on the other hand, it can attract the attention of people who otherwise probably wouldn't be at all interested in the facts. Of course, it would probably be rather condescending to send it to the chief executive!

Incidentally a table of these figures would be something like this:

LSS Company Plc: Progress in house-building (units)

1980	1981	1982	1983
300	500	700	150

Hardly worth the trouble to provide pictures? Well, the

LSS Company, Plc: Progess in house-building (units)

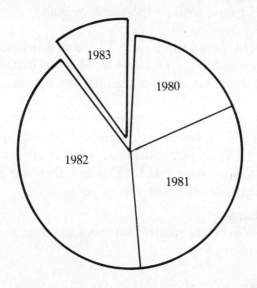

House-building for 1980-1983 (units)

pictures do have the edge on the bare figures if you're dealing with the totally disinterested type of user. The more dates and corresponding figures there are, the greater is the edge.

2. Pie-charts
Rather less condescending, these. Based on the fact that a circle has has 360° all we do is to measure-off with a protractor the number of degrees allocated to each segment. So a chart of this kind would tell us, say, that in four years 1980-1983 the percentage of houses built in each year were, respectively, 18, 30, 43, 9 (roughly).

This does mean that for some reason the four years are regarded as significant in respect of the contribution each one gives to the total of 1650 houses built.

Note that in the example on p.27, one particular year is singled out and 'highlighted' so that it looks like a slice of cake. Or we could shade a segment if we wished.

But we musn't overdo the number of 'slices' or segments or it becomes impossible to understand it easily (just like a complex table, in fact). Any way, very small items (e.g. year 1984, say, contributed 0,25% in a five year period) would hardly show up at all.

3. Bar-charts
These are (or can be made) more sophisticated, and there are a number of variants.

(a) The simple bar chart
Here is an example, and you can see that it doesn't really

do very much except give a straightforward picture of relative size. The bars or columns are of equal width; only the length differs.

LSS Company, Plc: Progress in House-building (units)

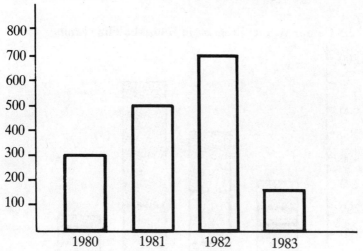

The same principle is used as in the pie-chart, except that instead of the segment of the 'pie' we have the bar.

This is at least much more accurate than either the picture or the pie-chart.

There is no real reason why the bars shouldn't be horizontal, instead of vertical. The only traditional objection is that time is usually represented on the line from left-to-right and not downwards or upwards.

(b) The component bar-chart
This one contains more information, since each bar is divided into segments to represent contributions to the total length of each bar. Like this:

LSS Company, Plc: Progress in House-building (units)

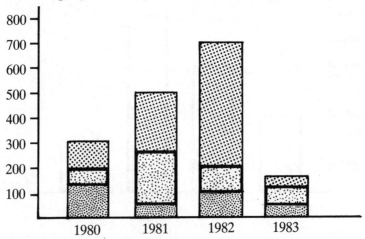

Obviously, you have to have more information to offer. Suppose we have three kinds of houses: so we would need a key to the chart, thus:

KEY

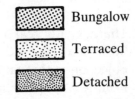

(c) The compound bar chart
Here each year is divided into separate bars rather than, as in (b), segments of a single bar. So this one emphasises the differences in the contributions to each total — which (b) actually has difficulty in doing. So here we see:

LSS Company, Plc: 5 Progress in house-building (units)

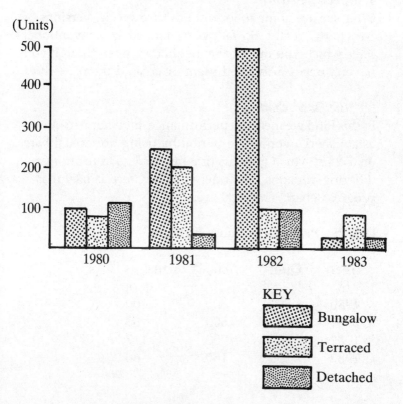

(d) The percentage bar chart
The difference between (b) and this one is that here we

have the bars broken up into *percentages*. So the vertical scale has to be from 0 to 100%. Each bar has to be the same total length because it is the *share* of each contribution to the total (100%) in which we are interested, not the actual figure.

4. Special charts

What we are going to look at now are special versions of bar-charts, really. So far we've looked at conventional ones which you must have met before, even though you haven't necessarily used them or created them.

(a) The Gantt chart

In this kind we measure performance, in relation to quotas established, over a time-period by using horizontal bars on a chart which gives us time-intervals. There are many differing versions. The one we show here is useful as a progress chart. The facts are:

LSS Plc. Progress in house-building

Year	Quota*	Actual*	Actual as % of quota
1980	300	300	100
1981	600	500	83
1982	600	700	117
1983	250	150	60

* units completed

LSS Company, Plc: 1980-1983 Building progress (units completed)

1980		1981		1982		1983	
Quota	Cum. Quota	Quota	Cum. Quota	Quota	Cum. Quota	Quota	Cum. Quota
300	300	600	900	600	1500	250	1750

1 year

2 years

3 years

4 years

KEY

Actual completions ●●●●●●

Cumulative figure ||||||||||||||||||

This is often built-up as the figures arise, and, especially if this is a chart telling people about progress, say, week-by-week, it can be a strong indication to those in charge of responsible teams what is happening. It doesn't pretend to give precise figures but it does say whether the quota or target was reached or not. You can devise your own version. If you want, you can only have a single horizontal row.

Notice that in 1982 the quota was exceeded for the year, and so the line had to double-up. You can see that the excess compensated for the shortfall in 1981 and so the cumulative line for three years revealed success.

Note also that each column-width represents a different quota figure so we're only concerned with the percentage of the quota obtained. The actual performance line for each year can only take up the full width if the full (100%) quota is achieved.

(b) The Zone chart
This one is used to show 'highs' and 'lows' in such things as prices, temperatures and anything else that can vary over a set time-period. This wouldn't apply to our house-building example we've been using, but here is the idea in relation to prices.

Here we have the minimum and maximum prices of a £1 share in a particular company, LSS plc. Raw material prices are often recorded in this way by purchasing officers.

LSS Company, Plc £1 share prices

Prices (£)

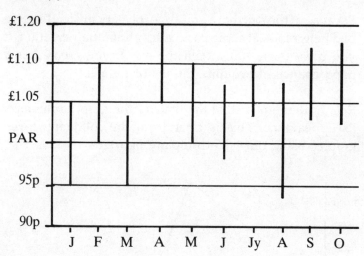

5. Graphs

If you decide to use a graph to present your statistics, *do* be careful. It's all too easy to succumb to the temptation of thinking that because you have some complicated figures you should use a graph. But the question really is, 'how much information can the reader get from the graph, and how easily?' The question is *not*: 'how much information can we get into this graph, and how easily?'

The theory is that people find a graph easier on the eye than tables. This may, or may not, be true. But they do often get very little from the graph (certainly not many figures, really) and remember far less. Of course, a dramatic line sweeping down, or up, is fairly memorable, but how many graphs have lines like that, anyway?

Because of the fact that a graph can be very misleading, we had better look at some basic rules about their creation. If you obey these rules, then the graph you create has a good chance of avoiding the major pitfalls:

Rule 1. Remember that the scale of the graph influences its appearance. This is clear from the following three graphs, using our LSS Company figures:

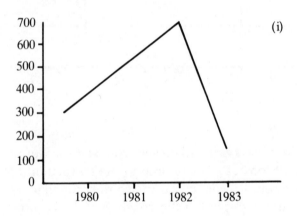

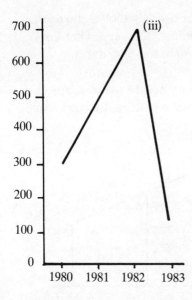

The scale varies horrifically, and the impact of the curve varies. The plottings are accurate enough, yet the average reader of the graphs would be completely confused. If presented with (ii) the *impression* carried away (and recalled) is that of a gradual climb followed by a nasty decline. If looking at (iii) the idea is of catastrophic plummetting down.

A helpful approach, therefore, is never to let the vertical axis be less than ⅔ or more than 100% of the horizontal axis. And use up the whole of the scale available. A good deal will depend upon the length of the period being looked at, and the quantities, but, by and large, the author has found this rough-and-ready concept useful.

Oh, yes, and *always* start your vertical scale with '0'. If the lowest number is large, then 'break' the scale, like this:

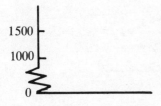

Rule 2. It is the shape of the graph-line which is the useful and important aspect: not absolute accuracy. That curve has to be neat, clearly distinguishable and definite.

You can also add finishing touches to your graph by putting in vertical lines which make reading-off the values easier, such as:

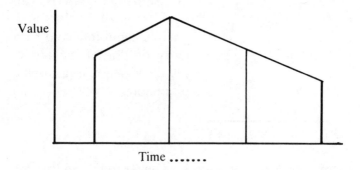

You can also, of course, adopt the '*multi-line graph*' idea, provided you don't overdo it and put in too many lines so that they become intermingled. The better kind look something like this one:

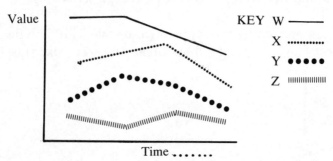

There are also *component graphs* which show how the top line (representing the total at a given time) is contributed to by the various parts:

LSS Company, Plc: Building progress, 1980-1983

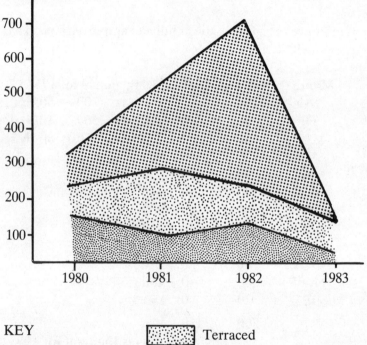

Not really very different from the component bar-chart is it? They are, by the way, sometimes referred to as 'band diagrams'.

6. The 'Z' chart

This is a rather special one. It provides three graph lines on the same structure, and they are:

- a moving annual total (MAT),
- the cumulative progress, and
- actual figures.

Our figures, relating to the familiar example we have used previously are:

Month	1982	1983	Moving annual total (MAT)	
JAN	50	0	650	i.e. $(700 - 50 + 0)$
FEB	40	0	610	i.e. $(650 - 40 + 0)$
MAR	60	5	555	i.e. $(610 - 60 + 5)$
APR	100	5	460	
MAY	90	20	396	
JUN	90	40	340	and so on
JUL	80	40	300	
AUG	50	10	260	
SEP	40	10	230	
OCT	40	20	210	
NOV	30	0	180	
DEC	30	0	150*	
	700	150		

* obviously, this is the total for 1983.

We simply took 1983 for our illustration, but it could have been any period for which figures are available, daily, weekly, monthly, quarterly, etc.

LSS Company, Plc: Progress in house-building 1983

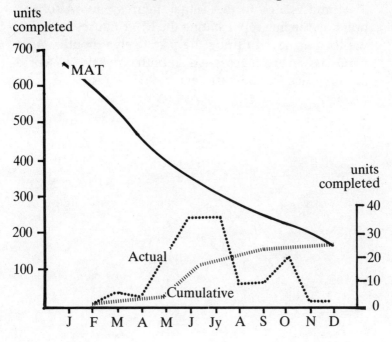

Since the whole point of this exercise is for the chart to be of use, look at it now and see what you see. Does it help towards an understanding of the situation more than the table would? By the way, you may not see from this one why it is a 'Z' chart. But if the point at which the MAT and cumulative lines meet were higher (i.e. if the fall were not so great) the three lines would form well, more or less, a 'Z' figure, but it does depend largely upon the scale you choose.

Note that the right hand axis has a completely different scale and related to the 'actual' figures only. Also, any point on the line representing the MAT figures relates to the total achieved during the past twelve months. As it happens, every successive month reveals a worse performance for the past year!

Checklist for presentation

1. WHAT STATISTICS HAVE TO BE PRESENTED?

(a) A mass of figures?
(b) For what reasons? What is to be shown?
(c) Regular, or ad hoc, one-off?
(d) With a report or narrative, or by themselves?

2. THE USERS

(a) Who are they? Experts in the area to which the statistics relate? Ignorant about the topic?
(b) Do they have to be motivated in some way to look at the statistics? Persuaded?
(c) Will they be able (and willing) to ask for clarification?

3. THE METHOD OF PRESENTATION

(a) What degree of approximation may be adopted?
(b) Can the statistics be summarised in any way?
  (i) If a time-period is involved, does every year have to be included, or could we quote, say, every second year?

(ii) Is there scope for the use of averages, percentages?

(c) How can we present the figures?

    (i) *Tables?*

How many (better several smaller ones than one large one)?

How many rows and columns?

What totals are necessary/desirable?

How can we simplify?

What title shall be given? Source? Units? Row and column headings?

How can the table(s) help the user? Are comparisons simple to make?

What is the user really expected to get out of the table(s)?

    (ii) *Illustrative diagrams?*

Pictures? (Would the users appreciate these? Do they allow enough detail?)

Pie-charts? (Or are there too many important figures?)

Bar-charts?

    Simple?

    Component?

    Percentage?

    Compound?

Special charts?

    Gantt (Do we want to stress progress?)

    Zone? (Are there 'highs and lows' in the figures?)

    (iii) *Analytical diagrams?*

Graphs? (Bearing in mind it is the USER who must derive benefit from this presentation,

what about the scale?) How useful would a graph be?
Simple graph?
Component graph?
Multi-line graph?
'Z' Chart?

(d) Would it be best to produce a mixture of some of these methods? Perhaps a table, supported by a bar-chart of some kind? Or by a graph?

What would be the advantage of combining these methods? Or, putting ourselves in the place of the user, would it be a waste of time (ours and theirs)?

'If only these were in a frquency table'

4. You are faced with a mass of figures : what are you going to do about it?

WHAT ABOUT REDUCING THE MASS TO WORKABLE SIZE?

Well, let's see how you could cut it down to a more comprehensible size so that it is less forbidding — and much more informative as well. Look at the unattractive mass of figures below, slipped onto our desk overnight. Mileage claims, these are, all 80 of them, for the month of April:

748	1,000	1,200	606	838	837	602	600
800	818	700	810	764	1,010	645	1,026
600	1,247	1,240	700	694	690	740	610
756	675	709	634	700	608	804	804
1,247	1,248	1,108	689	986	601	600	1,000
700	707	690	999	699	703	1,001	1,236
606	837	602	689	740	1,026	1,206	748
602	1,205	701	694	699	819	838	1,200
1,202	1,249	801	1,210	1,101	1,234	716	747
908	604	803	1,214	699	800	700	837

Not very informative, so what we need is order.

First of all, the simplest 'order' we can create here is by placing the numbers in some kind of *numerical* order (usually commencing with the lowest and ending with the highest value). So we would have:

	(f)		(f)		(f)		(f)		(f)		(f)		(f)
600	(3)	645	(1)	703	(1)	764	(1)	837	(3)	1,026	(2)	1,214	(1)
601	(1)	675	(1)	707	(1)	800	(1)	838	(2)	1,101	(1)	1,234	(1)
602	(3)	689	(2)	709	(2)	801	(1)	908	(1)	1,108	(1)	1,236	(1)
604	(1)	690	(2)	716	(2)	803	(1)	986	(1)	1,200	(2)	1,240	(1)
606	(2)	694	(2)	740	(2)	804	(2)	999	(2)	1,202	(1)	1,247	(2)
608	(1)	699	(3)	747	(3)	810	(1)	1,000	(2)	1,205	(1)	1,248	(1)
610	(1)	700	(5)	748	(5)	818	(2)	1,001	(1)	1,206	(1)	1,249	(1)
634	(1)	701	(1)	756	(1)	819	(1)	1,010	(1)	1,210	(1)		

THE USEFUL IDEA OF FREQUENCIES (f)

In addition to having information which now tells us that the lowest figure is 600 miles and the highest figure is 1,249 (what we refer to as a RANGE of 1,249 − 600 = 649 miles), we also know that certain of the mileages occur more than once. The figures in the brackets give us these repetitions and we refer to the 'frequency' of the occurrence of each number (f).

Certainly our figures are now ordered, but we can do better than this.

THE FREQUENCY TABLE

We can summarise the mass of data still further by using classes or categories within which the frequencies (mileages) fit. Our resultant frequency table could look like this:

LSS Plc
Mileage claims made, April, 19xx

Mileage claimed	f.	cumulative f.	cum.%
600 to under 750	39	39	48.75
750 to under 900	16	55	68.75
900 to under 1,050	9	64	80.00
1,050 to under 1,200	2	66	82.50
1,200 to under 1,350	14	80	100.00
	80		

These classes are really obtained by trial and error, but don't have less than 5 or more than 20. Do have the classes the same size as each other (in our example the class size is 150 miles claimed). Avoid 'open-ended' classes (e.g. Over 1,200) if possible.

Incidentally,you don't lose much by condensing the information like this. You still get the general picture of claims made ('two-thirds were under 900 miles' and so on) without having to wade through cost-ineffective morasses of digits. Note that all data can be treated like this. Contrast this table with our previous examples. In this version we're not concerned with the movement of data over time (time-series) but with data occurring during a fixed period of time.

You could also turn the 'cumulative' column of figures into a graph, if you think about it. It could look like the one opposite.

The axis on the right automatically gives you the percentage of the total achieved by what point. Why calculate this! The graph is officially called an 'ogive', or 'cumulative frequency curve'. It is also a 'less than' ogive, because the cumulative frequencies are plotted at the *upper limit* of the class intervals (the highest of point of each) and any point on the curve will give you the number of items (in this case claims) which have a value of less than the reading point on the horizontal axis. Broadly speaking, then (and there is no claim to precision here, merely to a good sensible rough number!) 75% of the claims made (60 in number) were less than 975 miles.

You can also compare the claims (or whatever) of another month by drawing the ogive of that month on the same graph. This gives you a quick overview which can be very illuminating.

LSS Company, Plc: Mileage claims, April, 19XX

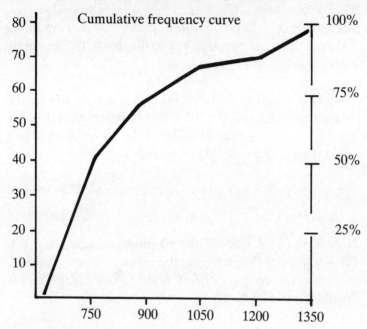

WHAT ELSE CAN YOU DO?

Produce 'averages'.

For business purposes there are three 'averages' which are in common use: the mean, the median and the mode. An average tries to pretend that it really represents, in a single figure, a whole set of figures. A useful idea if you know what it can and can't do!

1. The MEAN.

This is the most widely used and generally understood average. Yet, when we refer to the 'average man' or 'average woman' we don't actually have the mean in mind, but the mode (see later)!

To get the mean, as you well know, we simply add up the quantities and divide by the number of them. Our mileage claims add up to a total of 67,466 miles, as a matter of fact. The mileage claim for April is thus

$$\frac{67,466}{80} = 843.325 \text{ miles, or approximately 843 miles}$$

Now, don't look back at the 80 mileage claims, but just think what this single figure, the mean, tell you. Suppose you hadn't been given the 80 figures but only the mean. Would it convey much to you?

By itself, probably not. Well then, suppose you knew that the previous month had 80 claims, too, and that the mean for that month was 901 miles? would that help? Very generally, you would be inclined to think that the broad picture ('scatter' or 'dispersion') of the figure claims were very similar. In the absence of other information that would be a reasonable assumption to make.

Can we measure how representative the mean is?
Yes, we can, in a word. We can work out the average deviation of the figures from their mean: the *'absolute mean deviation'*. We simply take the mean figure from each of

the actual figures (all 80 of them) and then add up and find the 'mean deviation'. So we have:

600 − 843 = 243 (actually this repeated three times in the set of figures we have) ignoring the minus sign;

601 − 843 = 242 (only once in the set)

.... and so on until ....

1,249 − 843 = 406 (once only).

Our total deviations from the mean amount to: 14,073.

So, the mean absolute deviation is

$$\frac{14,073}{80} = 175.9, \text{ or } 176 \text{ miles.}$$

Be clear what we have done. We took the mean of our mileage claims and supported it by the average amount it deviates from the real figures themselves.

843 is the mean with an average deviation of 176 miles.

This is a very useful idea, but we can't use it in any maths calculations at a higher level because, for one thing, we ignored the minus signs. Also, this measure is hard work if you have a lot of fiddly figures with decimal points. Nevertheless it is very representative: it represents the dispersions of the data.

2. The MEDIAN

Now, although the arithmetic mean is the most familiar type of average, the median is a good alternative and very helpful.

The median is the middle figure of the set of figures when these are placed in ascending (or descending) order of value. So in our mileages you will be able to select the two (because we have an even number!) central ones as

756 and 764

In practice we usually take the right-hand number of these two, so we can call our median 764. If you wanted to be pedantic about it, you'd take the arithmetic mean of the two central figures, but, really this isn't neccessary. If you're making comparisons the important thing is not to adopt different ways of finding the median! Stick to the one method throughout.

3. The MODE

This is what we meant when we said that referring to 'the average man/woman' we had the mode, not the mean, in mind. The mode refers to the 'most commonly-met man/woman' who form the bulk of society

The mode, then, is the typical item, or value in a set of figures: the one which emerges more often than any of the others. In our mileage claims, 700 is the mode.

But there can't be a mode if all the figures are different! It is also possible to have more than one mode.

WHEN DO YOU USE WHAT?

Let's look at the three averages more closely:

Mean

Good points:
- easy to work out and understand (and that goes for people using your statistics, as well as yourself!);
- it uses *all the figures* and misses nothing out;
- it does have possibilities for further maths purposes.

Limitations:
- extreme values make it unreal (e.g. if our 80th) mileage claim had been 12,490 our mean would have been 984 miles, distorted by the one 'wayout' quantity and thus less representative of the whole group!);
- silly values can be the result of our calculation of the mean (e.g. the mean family size is 4.68!).

Median

Good points:
- it isn't hard for anyone to grasp as an idea;
  you can use it for measuring things which can't be measured mathematically;
- extreme values don't affect it at all;
- it is usually an actual item in the set;
- it is found by inspection, not calculation.

Limitations:
- you have to set out the data in ascending or decending value order before you can get the median;
- you can't use it for further maths treatment.

Mode

Good points:
- Extreme values don't affect it;
- it is found by inspection;
- it is an actual value.

Limitations:
- you have to set out the data;
- you can't use it for further maths treatment.

There isn't, therefore, any easy road to choosing which average you will use. It depends upon the figures, for one thing. You can actually *calculate* all three from a frequency table (which we looked at in the beginning of this Chapter).

The choice of which average to use also depends to a large extent on the purpose you have in mind. Perhaps the best way of looking at this is to take the example of a shoe shop. The mean size of the male foot wouldn't help the retailer very much. Indeed, if it were actually known, it probably wouldn't be a real size at all — perhaps just a point between two shoe-sizes. On the other hand, he would welcome information as to the most typical size (mode) and would be prepared to stock more of this size than of the others.

Again, market researchers love the mode. 'The average family uses TWITTO' signifies that this has more use than any other. And 'most cat owners prefer it' is another way of putting it.

The fact is, the mode may well summarise the characteristics of a group better than either the median or the mean could.

Perhaps it would help if you referred to the mean as more of an analytical kind of average, whereas the median and the mode are more descriptive.

ANY OTHER WAY OF SUMMARISING?

Yes, we can use *quartiles*.

These are really the items, respectively, which are one quarter and three-quarters along the row of figures placed in value order. Just as we selected the median, so we can select the first quartile (Q_1) and the third quartile (Q_3) — if you are wondering where number two is, that's really the median!

So, the Q_1 in our mileage claim list is 694, and the Q_3 is 1,001.

Let's look at it like this:

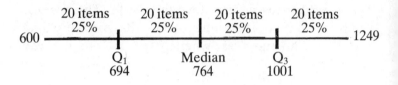

(Mean = 843 miles; mean deviation = 176 miles; Mode = 700; Range = 649 miles.)

You really have quite a neat 'armoury' in summary form which could tell the users of the statistics a good deal without wading through the mass of figures. Have a look at the idea and see how much you can extract yourself.

For instance:
>the first 20 claims were between 600 and 694 miles;
>the first 40 claims were between 600 and 764 miles;

or

>50% of the claims lay below 764 miles, and 50% above;
>20 claims (25%) were over 1,001 miles.

and so on. It depends on what you are looking for, doesn't it?

JUST A FINAL NOTE

You have been presented with a choice of 'statistical instruments'. Experiment with the ideas we have given you, discarding those which you don't like or don't feel are useful.

We haven't, by any standard, looked at even the majority of these ideas. For instance: you can produce the mean absolute deviation in respect of the median or the mode; there are other (much more complex) averages (e.g. the geometric), and there are other measurements (also more complex) of deviation (e.g. standard deviation). But what we have covered, so far, are the basic and very useful devices, which don't need a knowledge of maths as such.

5. Do your statistics show a special pattern

WHAT STATISTICS SHOW A PATTERN?

We have been dealing with two kinds of figures:

- *frequencies*, which are simply occurrences (obviously in our mileage claims example these occur or arise within a given time period, one month, April), and

- *time series*, where the figures vary *over the course* of a period of time (in our building progress example this was over four years).

Both of these types show some sort of pattern, and we begin by taking a look at

FREQUENCY PATTERNS

Here we want to find out about the 'spread' of the figures, the concentrations and so on. Taking our frequency table of mileage claims, we can show this pattern, whatever it may be, in the form of a diagram:

LSS Company, Plc: Mileage claims, April, 19XX

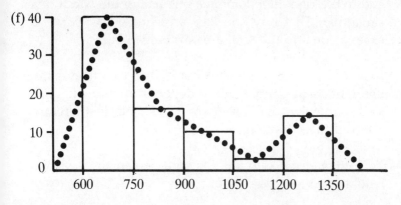

Like other types of presentation, this diagram does give you a clear chance of seeing, at a glance, the way the claims are distributed. Joining-up the points at the centres of the vertical bars gives us, in fact, a *'frequency distribution'*.

You can also make quick comparisons with other months if you want to by superimposing the respective curves for those months on to this one. Differences are soon seen. If you want to reduce all the figures per month to the same basis, then use percentage shares instead of actual frequencies (e.g. 49% of the claims fall into the first class, and so on).

In our diagram the vertical bars, together, are referred to usually as a *histogram* — not just another bar-chart! The curve drawn from the vertical bars (we call it a curve, but it is a very angular job in this case and it wouldn't be very practical to 'smooth' it) joins the horizontal axis to the left and to the right at a point just one half of the width of a single bar. That way, the total area under that curve is exactly equal to the total area of the five bars.

In real life, outside of the textbooks, you can meet many different shapes or patterns. It depends upon the figures. This particular one has two peaks and is therefore referred to as 'bi-modal'.

To compare, say, two months on a percentage basis we would produce this kind of result:

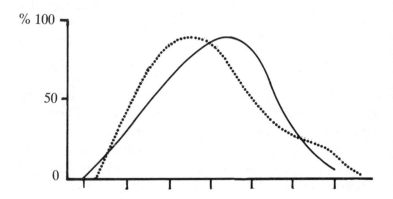

This kind of comparison tends to raise questions in our minds, such as why the difference? Auditors use these techniques a good deal.

TIME SERIES PATTERNS

We are now entering a rather more complex area of statistics. All figures relating to changes over a period of time are subject to various influences. These influences produce behavioural patterns which are likely to show themselves as:
- cycles,
- seasonal variations,
- catastrophies, phenomena,
- trends

Any other kind of behaviour will be 'random'.

(a) Cycles
These occur over a long period. Perhaps the most famous kind you've met are 'trade cycles', or 'business cycles', consisting of recurrent booms and slumps over couple of decades or so. But we are concerned with rather shorter periods here.

(b) Seasons
These are the ups and downs arising over a short (or even extremely brief) period. However, there are different types of 'seasons'. The commonest is the spring-summer-autumn-winter kind, but our business data may not be susceptible to this kind of influence in the same way.

'Seasons' concerned in the consumption of electricity, for instance, cover both 24 hours (high at breakfast-time, lunch-time and dinner-time; down between those times, and with a long time of 'off-peak' consumption between midnight to 0600 hours), and also the seven day stretches (consumption higher at week-ends). But there is also the conventional seasonal influence, with variations caused by 'Indian summers' and so on.

The lesson to be learned here is that the statistics have to be interpreted through knowledge of the business on hand and its characteristics and peculiarities.

We can 'extract' the seasonal variation by simple arithmetic. Let's take some typical sales data provided on a quarterly basis:

LSS PLC
Group products Sales (£'000s)
1980-1983

	1st Quarter	2nd Quarter	3rd Quarter	4th Quarter	TOTAL
1980	845	840	885	861	3,431
1981	862	850	899	895	3,506
1982	900	883	950	904	3,637
1983	930	920	952	949	3,751

To isolate the seasonal influence in the figures we have to
● get the moving average, and
● get the 'central' average, where we have an even number of seasons or time periods (we have 4 per year)

Bookmark

Dear Reader,
We hope that this
Management Update title is
helpful to you

Our aim in this and other titles
is to provide concise, practical
and up-to-date information on
key areas of concern to
commerce, industry and the
professions. Our publications
focus on:

- practice rather than theory

- helping the reader to
  understand concepts and
  apply them to solving
  everyday problems

- improving personal skills

- relevant and concise
  information rather than
  lengthy tomes.

We welcome comments and
suggestions from readers.
If you would like to be kept
informed of new titles, all you
need to do is to fill in your
name and address on the back
and return it to us.

**Management
Update Ltd.**

43 Brodrick Road
London SW17 7DX
Tel: 01-767 7542

Other **mu** titles

REPORT WRITING
Gordon Wainwright

**UNDERSTANDING YOUR
PENSION SCHEME**
D Hancox & J McMahon

GETTING YOUR NEXT JOB
John Hallett

**KNOW YOUR TRAINING
FILMS**
Directory & Reviews

BUSINESS RELOCATION
Hano Johannsen

**HOW TO DELEGATE
EFFECTIVELY**
L Seymour-Smith

**MAKING YOUR MEETINGS
MORE EFFECTIVE**
L Seymour-Smith

**UNDERSTANDING &
MAKING EFFECTIVE USE
OF STATISTICS**
L Seymour-Smith

**MAKING EFFECTIVE USE
OF TIME**
Bruce Austin

Name ....

Organisation ....

Address ....

This means we have to set out our figures in a way which facilitates these simple calculations:

	(£000's) Quarterly figures	(MA) Moving Average	(CA) Central Average	(SV) Seasonal variation
Note where	845			
the MA is	840			
placed; The	885	857.8	860.0	102.9
CA is back in	861	862.0	863.0	99.8
line opposite	862	864.5	866.0	99.5
the relevant	850	868.0	872.0	97.5
quarter's	899	876.5	881.0	102.0
figure.	895	886.0	890.0	100.6
	900	894.3	901.0	99.9
	883	907.0	908.0	97.2
	950	909.3	913.0	104.0
	904	916.8	921.0	98.2
	930	926.0	926.0	100.4
	920	926.5	932.0	98.7
	952	937.8		
	949			

Our *moving average* is obtained by taking the first 4 quarters and diving by 4, and then leaving out the first quarter and adding on the fifth quarterly figure. So we take four at a time, moving downwards one figure for each calculation:

e.g. $\dfrac{845 + 840 + 885 + 861}{4} = 857.8$, and then, next,

$\dfrac{840 + 885 + 861 + 862}{4} = 862.0$ and so on

You'll see that we have 'lost' a few figures on the way, i.e. we end up with 13 moving averages whereas we began with 16.

Our *central average* is achieved in the same kind of way, starting with the first two, calculating and then dropping the first figure and adding the third. So we have, for instance:

$$\frac{857.8 + 862.0}{2} = 860.0 \text{ (rounded), and then, next,}$$

$$\frac{862.0 + 864.5}{2} = 863.0 \text{ (rounded) and so on}$$

Again, yes, we did lose a figure, ending up with 12. What we really want here is the seasonal variation figures — these are obtained as follows:

$$\frac{\text{Quarterly figure}}{\text{CA}} \times 100;$$

e.g. first we have $\dfrac{885}{860} \times 100 = 102.9$ (rounded to one decimal)

then we have $\dfrac{861}{863} \times 100 = 99.8$

The whole point of specially aligning the MA's and the CA's is so that the relevant quarterly figures are matched opposite the relevant CA for this calculation.

Be careful about this, or you'll get chaos!

THE MEAN SV PATTERN

Setting these SV percentage variations out we get:

Quarter	1980	1981	1982	1983	Total	Mean SV**
1st	-	99.5	99.9	100.4	299.8	99.9
2nd	-	97.5	97.2	98.7	293.4	97.8
3rd	102.9	102.0	104.1	-	309.0	103.0
4th	99.8	100.6	98.2	-	298.6	99.5
						400.2

(** We divide the total by 3 because only 3 figures are there!)

Now, the total of these SV is 400.2, but, for reasons which concern percentage arithmetic they *should* only total 400. So, to be 'right and proper' and to get rid of the irritating + .2 which emerges from our rounding attempts, we will simply arbitrarily make an adjustment so that the four figures are now:

1st Quarter	99.8
2nd Quarter	97.7
3rd Quarter	103.0
4th Quarter	99.5
	400.0

But what are these figures? Believe it or not, they are the average way in which the quarterly figures have been behaving over the four years we looked at. 'On average' (mean-wise!) the highest quarter will be the third and the lowest the 2nd, and so on. We have used quarterly figures only because the figures pointed that way, but you can divide your time period into whatever elements you wish and treat your figures in the same way.

If the figures show any seasonal changes, then the SV would reflect this. But you can expect (provided that no influences disturb the pattern tomorrow!) your annual figures to follow the broad pattern indicated.

MONITORING YOUR PATTERN

As new figures come in, you can recalculate, using the latest four quarters and leaving out the first year's. If there is a difference in the mean SV pattern, then take a look at the latest year because something will have been disturbing it. In fact, this monitoring function is a very good reason for carrying out the SV calculations. It is a way of alerting you to something which you didn't see before.

You can also 'remove' the seasonal pattern's influence from the latest figures. Suppose we have 1984 quarters:
1984: (1) 1,200; (2) 1,100; (3) 1,230; (4) 1,188
We can convert these figures (deseasonalise) or seasonally adjust them by

$$\frac{\text{Quarterly figure}}{\text{SV}} \times 100$$

So, we have:

(1), $\dfrac{1,200}{99.8} \times 100 =$ Adjusted figure
1,202.4

(2), $\dfrac{1,100}{97.7} \times 100 = 1,125.9$

(3), $\dfrac{1,230}{103} \times 100 = 1,194.2$

(4), $\dfrac{1,188}{99.5} \times 100 = 1,194.0$

What you now have is the real situation which underlies the figures. The real behaviour in this case is that the sales have apparently tended to flatten-out, but it was actually upwards in the first two quarters.

MAKE A GRAPH COMPARISON

See what you can make of the graph on page 70, giving the actual figures and the *central average* figures:

The point about this graph is that you can see how relatively fluctuating the actual sales line is compared with the line which gives you the moving average (yes, it is actually the 'central average', but that IS a moving average , too, and it is flatter due to the

**LSS Company, Plc: Group products subsidiary.
Sales (£000's) 1980-1983**

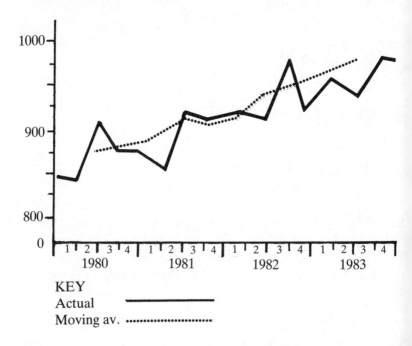

arithmetic process). Really, the dotted line gives you an indication of the overall trend, but more of that idea in the next Chapter.

You could, if you wished, produce a graph based upon the 'deseasonalised' figures, too.

6. How do you know the trend?

WHAT IS A TREND?

It's somewhat old fashioned now to refer to 'secular' trend, but it used to be called that to show that we were dealing with a longish rather than a short time period. Nowadays, anyway we are just as interested in either period of time so we refer to 'trend' simply as a general upward or downwards movement of figures.

Whereas we talk about trends in everyday conversation (e.g. to worse behaviour, more and more cars on the road, higher supermarket prices,) in statistical terminology we imply far less vagueness when we use the word.

Here we are not concerned with specifically mathematical techniques. It suffices therefore to point out that in some sets of figures we have to cope with 'curvilinear trend' which has to be dealt with in a fairly sophisticated way (and is best left to the computer anyway!) Here, we are going to look at linear trends, i.e. those which can be shown as straight lines.

'Can you see the trend clearly?'

DO WE HAVE A CHOICE OF METHODS?

Yes, we do. Here are the basic ones:

- 'Freehand' method,
- 'Selected points' method,
- 'Semi-average' method,
- 'Least squares' method.

1. Freehand

In this one we look carefully at a graph of the figures, and then we draw, freehand, a straight line which we believe to represent reasonably well the underlying movement of the values. It would be a good idea to use a transparent ruler and move it about until we think we've found the ideal beginning and end, and the line slope.

Once we've done our line we can then read on the vertical scale the point where it begins and finishes, so that we now know the 'rate of climb' (or otherwise) of the values. Thus we'd have something like £2,000 at the beginning (say, 1975) and perhaps £3,800 at the finishing point of our line (say, in 1984) so the rate of climb in this case would be £200 per year, or, if you prefer it, the average (mean) change of value per time unit.

Yes, when we are experts in our fields we can probably produce a very good freehand line — the more so, of course, when the figures don't differ very much above and below that line! But this method is, by definition, subjective. Indeed, take any two people and they will tend to draw rather different freehand lines.

So, if you are a beginner in this game, and if the figures do fluctuate a great deal, don't use this method!

2. Selected points
This is one stage beyond the previous method discussed. We select two points in the series of figures.

We should choose ones near the beginning and near the end which are fairly representative or characteristic, of the figures in hand.

As before, we would take the difference between the two chosen points and also divide by the number of 'time units' which separate them.

Suppose our figures were set out like this:

Year	Sales £000's	X		Value of trend
1975	1,860	−1		1,727.2
1976	2,000*	0		2,000.0
1977	2,408	1	(£2,000 + £272.8)	2,272.8
1978	2,806	2	(2,272.8 + £272.8)	2,545.6
1979	3,000	3	and so on	2,818.4
1980	3,431	4		3,091.2
1981	3,506	5		3,364.0
1982	3,637*	6		3,636.8
1983	3,751	7		3,909.6
1984	4,718	8		4,182.4

The calculation is: $\dfrac{3{,}637 - 2{,}000}{1982 - 1976}$ = £272.8 (thousands)

The 'value of trend' items are obtained by adding, in this example, 272.8 to the first selected part as you go down the column. The result is a column of figures which constitute your trendline.

This method is useful in that it is a quick *approximation* of the trend. However, it is still dependent on *subjective* judgement to determine where the two points are to be (in this example the asterisks indicate them).

3. Semi-averages
This method requires us to divide the series of figures into two equal parts and then calculate the mean for each. The layout would be:

Year	Sales (£000's)	Semi-average
1975	1,860	
1976	2,000	
1977	2,408	2,415
1978	2,806	
1979	3,000	
1980	3,431	
1981	3,506	
1982	3,637	3,809
1983	3,751	*We can now produce a simple graph, joining up*
1984	4,718	*these two points.*

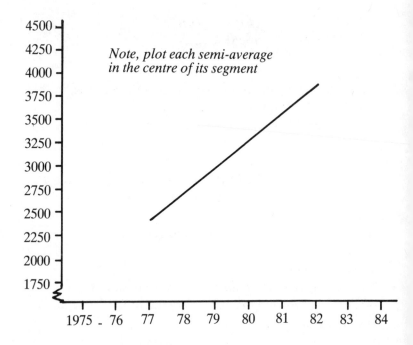

Note, plot each semi-average in the centre of its segment

This method isn't subjective like the other two. Our trendline's slope will depend upon the gap betwen the values of the two semi-averages, which were calculated from the original figures. Each mean is intended to be representitive of the half of the series to which it relates. By the way, if you have an odd number of years or other periods, drop out the middle one and pretend it doesn't exist.

But the arithmetic mean, as you already know, has an inherent flaw in that it is always affected by extreme values. So, if these exist in either half of the series, then the mean will mislead. If, say, one half's sales (or whatever) are affected by a strike, then the resultant line just isn't very representative of the whole series.

The briefer the time period the semi-average represents, the greater this difficulty is.

4. Least squares.
In theory this idea looks complex but it really isn't. It's quite simple, although it is a form of 'regression analysis' which sounds daunting. What we are going to do, is fit a straight line through the series of figures we have been working on in this Chapter.

In fact, it would be easier for you if you were to accept a straightforward formula:

$$y = a + bd$$

Take a look at this chart:

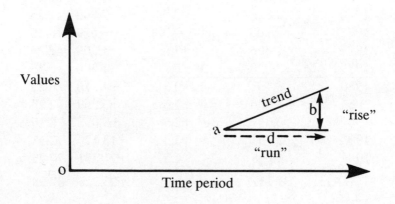

In our formula:

y   is the value we want to find out;
a   is the arithmetic mean of the series (put in the centre
     of the time period:
b   is the 'rise', i.e. the extent of the change in value over
d   which is the 'run', the fixed time period.

In fact what we are looking for is the length of the three
sides of the triangle, so that we know the hypotheneuse of
it (which will give us our trend).

Using our example again, we set the figures out, as
before:

Year	Sales (£000's) y	Time deviations d	yd	d^2
1975	1,860	−4.5	−8,370	20.25
1976	2,000	−3.5	−7,000	12.25
1977	2,408	−2.5	−6,020	6.25
1978	2,806	−1.5	−4,209	2.25
1979	3,000	−0.5	−1,500	0.25
1980	3,431	+0.5	+1,716	0.25
1981	3,506	+1.5	+5,259	2.25
1982	3,637	+2.5	+9,093	6.25
1983	3,751	+3.5	+13,129	12.25
1984	4,718	+4.5	+21,231	20.25
TOTALS	31,117		+23,329	82.50

We have, as before, divided our figures into equal parts. If we find we have an odd number of figures, then we DO NOT (as in the semi-averages) leave the centre one out. We would simply regard this middle one as the centre of the set and the absolute centre would be midyear (30th June). In this case, from that centrepoint to the middle of the year before it would be 1 whole year (i.e. our "d" column would give −1 and not −0.5).

However, we have an even number here and so the centrepoint must be at the end of a year (as it happens, 31st December, 1979). From that point to the middle of the year, going backwards in time, is obviously a distance of half a year, so we get in our 'd' column '−0.5'. From the same centrepoint to the middle of the previous year (1978) is therefore "−1.5", and so on.

What we do now is:

1. Get the arithmetic mean of the series: $\dfrac{31,117}{10} = 3,112$

2. Divide the total of the column yd by the total of the column d;
$$\frac{+23,329}{82.50} = 282.8$$

3. Our trend is:
$$£3,112,000 \pm (£282,800 \times d).$$

Remember our diagram? The mean is the centre. So the 'rise' is 282.8, per year and the time-period (d) is the number of years. This means that we can set out our trend as:

	Trend (£000's)	
1975	1,839.4	i.e. 3,112 − (282.8 x 4.5)
1976	2,122.2	i.e. 3,112 − (282.8 x 3.5)
1977	2,405.0	i.e. 3,112 − (282.2 x 2.5)
1978	2,687.8	i.e. 3,112 − (282.8 x 1.5)
1979	2,970.6	i.e. 3,112 − (282.8 x 0.5)
1980	3,253.4	i.e. 3,112 + (282.8 x 0.5)
1981	3,536.2	i.e. 3,112 + (282.8 x 1.5)
1982	3,819.0	and so on
1983	4,101.8	
1984	4,384.6	

Should the net figure total for the yd column be a minus, then this means that the trend is downwards, not upwards.

This method obviously needs rather more trouble taken over it than the others, but as you will see in the next Chapter, the extra degree of sophistication may well be worth it. Yes, there are more mathematical methods, but in the overwhelming majority of cases, the least squares method is sufficient for all practical purposes.

7. So you believe in the crystal ball, too?

FORECASTING IS NOT A NEW IDEA

In business, forecasting is hardly a new concept. The businessman has to forecast even if the whole of his output is sold before it is actually produced. In general, of course, firms produce in anticipation of demand and therefore forecast demand and selling prices.

But what *is* new about forecasting (well, relativly new) is the general business approach to 'scientific' forecasting, rather than intuition and plain guesswork. Still, forecasts, even in highly scientific areas (meteorology is a classic case!) are very often wrong.

ALL forecasts have to be based upon certain assumptions which have to be regarded as constraints (e.g. official policy over the short-period, say, or the impact of ecconomic measures in the economy over the long-period.)

'So you believe in the crystal ball too?'

HOW SHOULD YOU SET ABOUT FORECASTING?

Be methodical about it. The Chart on p.84 shows you the various stages you could adopt, and we'll go into them in detail now:

1. Decide the nature of the forecast

a   What exactly is to be forecast?
    What units are to be used? Is this quite clear?

b   How far ahead are you to forecast?
    Next week? Next year? Five, ten, twenty years ahead?
    Obviously, the further ahead you forecast, the greater the probability that you'll be wrong (very wrong, that is). But we still have to forecast long periods ahead in, say, corporate planning.

c   What past data will be used in the calculation?
    How far back will you need to go?
    To some extent this depends upon:
    ● the availability of the data
    ● their reliability,
    ● whether, beyond a certain date, specific events have caused the figures to be untypical (e.g. general strike in the industry), or
    ● whether influences existed in the past which have now altered.

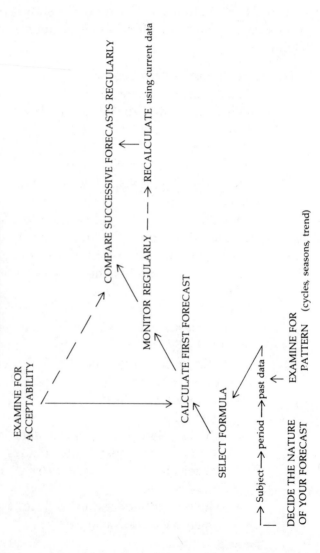

BASIC FORECASTING STAGES

EXAMINE FOR
ACCEPTABILITY

COMPARE SUCCESSIVE FORECASTS REGULARLY

MONITOR REGULARLY — — → RECALCULATE using current data

CALCULATE FIRST FORECAST

SELECT FORMULA

→ Subject ──→ period ──→ past data

EXAMINE FOR
PATTERN (cycles, seasons, trend)

DECIDE THE NATURE
OF YOUR FORECAST

2. Examine past data for pattern
Analyse as we did our time series figures earlier, find out what influences exist(ed) and what the seasonal pattern (if any exists) and the trend are.

Clearly, 1c and 2 are linked. You have to stike a balance between using figures which stretch back far enough to present a picture of patterns, and yet not so far into history that the influences existing then don't apply now.

3. Select formula
More about this later in this Chapter.

4. Calculate your first forecast and then

5. Examine for acceptability
You MUST look at your forecast in the light of experience and common sense.

Does your forecast seem, on the face of it, reasonable?

6. Monitor your forecasts regularly

This monitoring approach is very useful. There are two aspects to it:

(a) As time goes by and new figures arise, recalculate your forecast. Look at the forecast you made previously, say, two years ahead, and this new one (after, say, a year's figures have emerged) now relates to one year ahead. How different is it? Did you, for instance, forecast that in 1987 you'd sell

1,000,000 tons of Waffle? What does your new forecast for 1987 say? 500,000 tons?

The really important thing is not really that the two forecasts disagree, but WHY they disagree. What influences did the new figures have upon the calculation and why?

(b) Irrespective of the nature of the forecast itself, the process of keeping a watchful eye on the data can often alert you to opportunities, potential difficulties and so on which you may not have noticed just by looking at the figures.

HOW WILL YOU CALCULATE THE FORECAST?

You can, if you wish, use freehand, selected points or semi-averages if you want to. But the first two, you will recall, were branded as somewhat subjective and the semi-average method as approximate (largely due to the nature of the two arthmetic methods used).

All in all there are two reasonable approaches we can adopt.

- moving averages, and
- least squares.

Both of these we have already outlined in Chapter 5.

1. Moving averages

In our discussion about seasonal variation we found ourselves involved in what we call a moving average and a central average. In our Z Chart, earlier, we used a moving annual total (MAT) — if we'd divided each of the figures we derived for that MAT by 12, we'd have obtained a moving average (same shape, slope, but lower down on the axis!).

For forecasting purposes, we would use obtain the moving average (using whatever "pattern" of weeks or months we considered useful - so we might 'average by dividing by three, or nine months, or whatever seemed suitable) and then try to extend the smooth plotted line into the future.

There are several types of moving average, by the way, and the one we have used before is the 'linear' type. There is also the 'progressive' moving average which averages all the new figures as they arrive. So, we would, if we had monthly figures, add the new month's figures and then divide by the number of months including the new month. E.g.

First average: $\dfrac{\text{Jan} + \text{Feb}}{2}$

Second average: $\dfrac{\text{Jan} + \text{Feb} + \text{Mar}}{3}$

Third average: $\dfrac{\text{Jan} + \text{Feb} + \text{Mar} + \text{Apr}}{4}$

However, the problem is that all moving averages are rather slow to adapt to a change in trend. All in all, they're simple to understand and work out, but they can only be used for short period forecasting — say four years of monthly forecasting (48) used to forecast perhaps up to six months ahead.

2. Least squares forecasting

Let's set out our figures and our least squares trend we met in the previous Chapter, again:

Year	Trend in Sales (£000's)	Actual
1975	1,839.4	1,860
1976	2,122.2	2,000
1977	2,405.0	2,408
1978	2,687.8	2,806
1979	2,970.6	3,000
1980	3,253.4	3,431
1981	3,536.2	3,506
1982	3,819.0	3,637
1983	4,101.0	3,751
1984	4,384.6	4,718

Now we know that our trend rises be £282,800 annually. So, if we want a forecast, based upon this trend, for, say, 1985, then all we have to do is add this 'instalment' to the 1984 figure.

Our 1985 forecast is therefore
£4,667,400
Incidentally, if we didn't want to set out the individual figures of the trend we would simply use the formula:
£3,112,000 + (£282,800 x 5.5)
for the 1985 forecast, exactly as we would do for a trend figure relating to a given year. If we wanted the forecast to relate to 1990, then the calculation would be:

£3,112,000 + (£282,800 x 10.5) = £6,081,400

HOW RIGHT WOULD THE FORECAST BE?

We can't tell how accurate our forecast is going to be, no matter how sophisticated, computerised, advanced and complex our forecasting methods are. We *can*, however, get a rough idea, based upon the sort of calculation we have just carried out. But the author does have a friend who held Premium Savings Bonds for fifteen years and won absolutely nothing and who, lived next door to a man who held a few for a year and won a top prize. Yes, and he also knows someone who has twice been struck by lightening. In otherwords, whatever will be will be!

To get our broad idea, we look at the differences bewteen the actual sales (or whatever) and our trend line figures:

FORECASTING CALCULATION AND MONITORING SCHEME

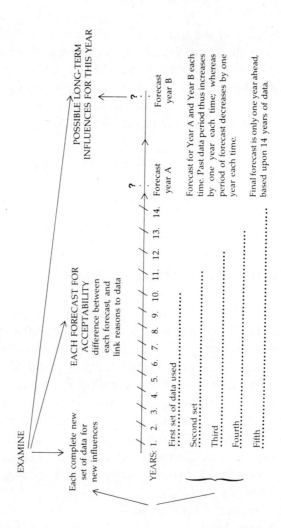

EXAMINE

POSSIBLE LONG-TERM
INFLUENCES FOR THIS YEAR

EACH FORECAST FOR
ACCEPTABILITY
difference between
each forecast, and
link reasons to data

Each complete new
set of data for
new influences

?

?

YEARS: 1. 2. 3. 4. 5. 6. 7. 8. 9. 10. 11. 12. 13. 14.   Forecast   Forecast
year A   year B

First set of data used

Second set

Third

Fourth

Fifth

Forecast for Year A and Year B each
time. Past data period thus increases
by one year each time; whereas
period of forecast decreases by one
year each time.

Final forecast is only one year ahead,
based upon 14 years of data.

Trend minus actual*	Difference as % of trend
−21	−1.1
+122	+5.8
−3	−0.1
−118	−4.0
−29	−0.9
−178	−5.0
+30	+0.1
+182	+4.8
+351	+8.6
−333	−7.6

So, we have the range of 'error', and we see that it is from −7.6 to +8.6, that is, covering a total of 16.2%.

There's little point in getting into this any deeper by taking a mean % error, and you know that the mean can be misleading anyway. What we have done is to provide ourselves with an advance warning that the margin of inaccuracy could be, if we are pessimistic (i.e. cautious!) about — in terms of out 1985 forecast, say:
£4,667,400 + 8.6% down to −7.6%, or roughly
£5,068,000 to £4,313,000

It would be a good idea to adopt that monitoring process, wouldn't it and see just how accurate your forecast is? That way, if you are forecasting three years ahead you can forecast for one year ahead as well and make this comparison when the new data arrive. In any case, we say again, the business environment could change. Common sense must always be brought to bear on forecasting!

8. Two sets of figures seem linked in some way: can we measure this?

THE ANSWER IS

YES we can, *but* we can only determine the degree of linkage or 'correlation' which we know actually does exist. We *could* find some statistical link between the number of girl babies born in Cairo during the years 1970-1980 and the output of Yorkshire coalfields in the previous decade, but the whole thing would be ridiculous. Well, wouldn't it?

Now, where two quantities vary in such a manner that movements in one are accompanied by movements in the other, there is some correlation. You can think of many instances: an increase in the issue of TV licences accompanied by a decrease in cinema attendances; or an increase in rainfall and in increase in the production of, say, barely per acre. Note that in the first example one set of figures increased and the other decreased. In correlation we don't have to have both sets travelling upwards or downwards.

ARE THERE ANY SNAGS?

Of course! Just because two sets of figures appear to move in sympathy, this does NOT ALWAYS show that there is cause and effect. The changes may be due to an influence common to both of them. Cases like the one concerning Cairo and Yorkshire, quoted above, are referred to as 'spurious correlation' — a better term is 'rubbish'.

THE IDEA OF 'SIMPLE CORRELATION'

We will leave the more complicated forms of correlation to the maths people. Here we deal with relatively simple issues which will be useful to you.

We can get a rough idea of the correlation between two kinds of units (say, weight and height of human beings) if we plot the figures in the form of a *'scatter' diagram*. This is only a question of plotting all the known values on a graph, so we get:

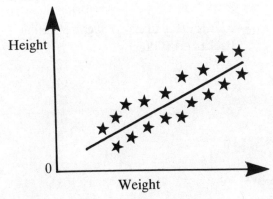

In technical terms this is called positive linear correlation, but the theme is that all points lie, more or less, in a straight line which extends upwards from left to right. It would be negative linear correlation if it travelled downward from left to right.

If the points scattered all over the place i.e. at random we would say there was no correlation.

THE CORRELATION COEFFICIENT

This is a much more tedious calculation but it does produce a single figure — a coefficient — which tells you a lot about the linkage. We are going to use very simple figures because we want to illustrate the general idea.

Suppose we have a factory which produces gears and the management considers that the cost of the output is directly related to the quantity produced. They have figures of costs and output for half a year:

		x Number of units Produced (000's)	y Cost (£000's)
JAN		8	12
FEB		9	14
MAR		6	10
APR		10	16
MAY		2	6
JUN		7	11
	Total	42	69

What correlation exists, then between cost and output?

We carry out these steps:
1. Multiply *each* cost by the relevant output, so we get:
    96, 126, 60, 160, 12, 77 = 531 (Total of xy)

2. Total the output units, and total the cost: square each total:
    units = 42 (squared = 1,764), (Total of x)^2
    and costs = 69 (squared = 4,761). (Total of y)^2

3. Square each value of the outputs and get the total. Then do the same for costs. We get:
    units: 64, 81, 36, 100, 4, 49 = 334 (Total x^2)
    costs: 144, 196, 100, 256, 36, 121 = 853. (Total y^2)

We know that there are 6 values of each, output and cost, so we'll call this n.

We now have a formula to follow in order to get the correlation coefficient:

$$\frac{n\Sigma xy - \Sigma x \Sigma y}{\sqrt{[n\Sigma x^2 - (\Sigma x)^2][\nu\Sigma y^2 - (\Sigma y)^2]}}$$

(Σ is, you may recall the convenient symbol meaning sum of.)

In plain figurework this boils down to:

$$\frac{6(531) - (42)(69)}{\sqrt{[6(334) - 1,764)][6(853) - 4,761]}}$$

which comes down to:

$$\frac{3,186 - 2,898}{\sqrt{(2,004 - 1,764)(5,118 - 4,761)}}$$

and thus to:

$$\frac{288}{\sqrt{(240)(357)}}$$

$$= \frac{288}{\sqrt{85,860}}$$

and finally,

$$\frac{288}{293} = 0.98$$

The correlation ceofficient is 0.98

What does this mean?

Well, the measures may be interpreted like this:
    0 = no correlation at all;
    −1 = perfect negative correlation; and
    +1 = perfect postive correlation.

The coefficent CANNOT be lower than −1 or higher than +1. 0.74 would thus show that there is a fairly high degree of correlation between production levels and costs.

Obviously, this approach to correlation is rather tedious (especially as there will be large numbers and possibly decimal places as well) but it isn't hard to follow. The use of symbols, you'll notice, does make following the formula much easier.

9. What do you know about using statistical sources?

WHAT SOURCES, WHERE?

Where do we look for the statistical sources we need?

Three categories are available to us: internal, external and direct. We'll deal with this last one in chapter 10.

1. Internal
Figures which exist, or can be found, within our organisation are an obvious starting point. This doesn't mean that we can get everything we want from this internal source, but usually it does provide a starting-point for us.

Much information is contained in personnel records, ledgers, in the various departments and divisions — whether this is held in physical files in filing-cabinets or in the form of computerised store.

The big advantage of internal statistics is that we can still get further information from people who were responsible for recording it in the first place. We can seek amplification and so on.

On the other hand, the figures are obviously limited and we can't use them as indicators of other organisational performances.

2. External

We are usually obliged, in any case, to look for outside sources, and there is no shortage of them for most areas of inquiry!

First of all, we have to accept that most of the general statistics available to us aren't specially prepared for us and our specific investigation! Rarely can we find out exactly what we want to know, immediately. We'll probably find we have to use some of the ideas already looked at in this book.

But, before we begin all this, we ought to have some kind of logical sequence or plan for using these external figures. We begin with the decision to use them and go right through to the end stage. The Chart on the next page will help here: it shows that the stages are:

● Determine the actual objectives.
● Choose the figures from the source available.
● Check the figures.
● Extract and simplify.
● Present the statistics.

Let's take a look at the implications.

1. Objectives

Well, if we don't know what we want, we aren't going to

Questions to assist in the use of external statistics

(1) Objective(s)	(2) Choose source	(3) Check figures	(4) Extract/simplify	(5) Presentation
What is it we are actually seeking?	Where do we find the figures?	Are these figures suitable?	In what way can we get at the facts?	In what form?
	Official? Semi-official? Private? International?	ARE they: the best we can get? Standard? Complete Comprehensive? Free of mistakes? Comparable? Provisional? and What changes occur? What period is covered?	Should we: use averages? Ratios? Percentages? Index numbers? Omit some years?	What is best? Tables? Graphs? Charts? A Mixture?

get it, whatever it is! In other words this is so obvious that we just couldn't forget to check our objective(s).

If the whole point of the exercise is, say, to find out how society is 'progressing' or how 'efficient' an industry is, then we do have a few problems of definition ahead. If we want to check up on a crime rate in the UK cities, we have to make sure what 'crime rate' does mean (reported crimes? unsolved? petty theft? murder? suspected crimes?). And while we're about it we do know what a 'city' is, don't we?

2. Choose figures from sources available

We're talking here of external sources, of course, and there are many. Basic categories here are:

Official

There is a Stationery Office publication (free) called 'Government Statistics - a brief guide to sources' which you can get from The Press & Information Services, The Central Statistical Office, Great George Street, LONDON, SW1P 3AQ.

The GSS (Government Statistical Service) comprises the statistics divisions of all major departments and has two large collecting agencies (the Business Statistics Office and the Office of Population Census and Surveys) and the system is coordinated by the CSO (Central Statistical Office).

Although the GSS exists to serve the needs of the Government, business statistical needs (especially marketing) are also met to a great extent. The statistics are not purely economic in nature.

Perhaps the best known of official sources is the 'Annual Abstract of Statistics' (CSO).

> *Semi-official*
> These are bodies supported partly by Government funds, e.g. NIESR (National Institute for Economic and Social Research).
> *Private*
> This includes a wide range of bodies such as the Trade and Professional Associations, Universities and commercial organisations like the Econonmist Intelligence Unit.
> *International*
> These include the official statistics provided by the Governments of other countries, and the world or regional bodies such as the United Nations, the EEC (which has an information office in London), the World Bank Group and the International Monetary Fund (IMF).

3. Check figures

It may be that we choose all our statistics from one single source, or, it could be that we have to use several different ones. What we have to make sure of is *consistency*.

a Are they the best we can get?

'Best' means cost effective, taking both time and cost into account.

b Are they standard?

What we really mean here is are they reliable statistics or are they suspect? What is the standing of the source? How authoritative? Some of the data provided through private bodies (perhaps as a by-product of some research or other) may be inadequate for our purpose due to their limited scope and budget restrictions.

c Are they complete?
Are any of the figures excluded (perhaps due to the fact that when the source was published they weren't ready?)

d Are they comprehensive?
Examine the definitions involved: do they cover the whole range of our needs?

e Are they free of mistakes?
It isn't very likely at all the figures you take from any source, official or otherwise, will be free of error. This is because there can be typographical mistakes as well as simple human errors of other types. So there can be:

● basic mistakes in adding, subtracting, etc.,
● incorrect'rounding',
● printing errors giving 'rogue' figures.

f Are they comparable?
Especially if we are using a number of different sources, we can meet incomparabilities and incompatibilites. A classic example (given earlier in this Chapter) is that of "£billions". Another is GB and UK. They aren't the same. And is the US tax year the same as that of the UK? And what about figures expressed in money terms and/or real terms?

g Are the figures provisional?
Or are they firm? Rapidly, punctually published figures may well be (considerably) modified at a later date. Take a look at, say the 'Blue Books on National Income & Expenditure' which were published in 1980, 1982, 1984. See the changes in quite important figures?

h What changes occur?
Quite apart from the changes implicit in (g), there could be alterations to definitions. And, of course, things like geographical boundaries e.g. Parlimentary constituencies and Local Authority areas may well have changed.

i What period is covered?
Here we refer to our objective(s) again. Complete figures which relate to, say, only five or six prevous years may have to be used together with less detailed data relating to, say, a decade.

j Extract and simplify
The whole and series figures with which we are now faced, having decided upon our source, will very probably have to be 'treated' so that the mass of what is now our primary data is actually usable and understandable.

This means that we have to bring into action some of the ideas already referred to in previous Chapters. We can also be original (if we're certain that we are not overstepping the mark a bit!) provided we do obey the rules.

Some of the treatment we can give to a mass of statistics may include:

- *Missing out some years.* Well, do we really *have* to include every single year of the past two decades? Why not perhaps miss out every second year? Or simply quote statistics for - say - 1965, 1970, 1975, 1980 if that is sensible.

- *Adding some figures together.* If we are faced with, say, statistics relating to ages of the population which are in the format of 5-10, 10-15, 15-20, etc., then we can restrict the number of the classes by adding e.g. 5-15, etc.

- *Using averages.* Don't forget the advantages (and disadvantages) of the mean, median and mode.

- *Percentage conversions.* Here you have quite a wide choice e.g. % increase or decrease over the period of a year; or % shares.

- *Rounding.* Yes, but go carefully.

5. Presentation
How? And, of course, why? Not forgetting to whom?

Our Chapters 2 and 3 put you on the road to sucess there!

As a final note here's, a brief guide to some established sources:

THE ANNUAL ABSTACT OF STATISTICS
This is a major reference work, bringing together most business and economic statistics published by the CSO. Full definitions are provided.

THE MONTHLY DIGEST OF STATISTICS
An abbreviated version of the Annual Abstract published every month.

FINANCIAL STATISTICS
Financial/monetary UK statistics on such aspects as:
banking
rates of interest
central and local government
balance of payments.

DEPARTMENT OF EMPLOYMENT GAZETTE
Monthly, providing data on prices and labour, including:
employment/unemployment
wage rates
retail prices
work stoppages.

ECONOMIC TRENDS
Monthly statistics and graphs on areas such as:
labour
external trade
production
investment
earnings, wages, prices.

THE BLUE BOOK ON NATIONAL INCOME AND EXPENDITURE
An annual publication, giving:
Gross National Product (analysed into sections)
Gross National Income (by sources)
Gross National Expenditure (by category).

THE FINANCIAL TIMES
This newspaper, together with other publications (investment publications, for instance) gives such information as: the FT Actuaries All-Share Index and
The FT Industrial Share Index.

10. The truth about surveys

THE DIRECT METHOD OF GETTING THE FACTS

Previously we looked at using internal and external sources of your statistics. Now we come to the hard work! Getting the facts yourself. Obviously, if it is claimed in an advertisement that '8 out of 10 dogs said their owners preferred it' then somebody must at one time or another have communicated with the dogs.

There is no earthly reason why you shouldn't conduct a simple survey yourself, given that you (again) follow the rules, We can give you general outlines here, and, if the approach is relevant to your needs you can then follow it up in greater detail by reading-up further approaches in which, say, sampling is involved.

THE SURVEY

By this term we mean the actual way adopted of getting the information to be researched. Surveys aren't carried out exclusively by businesses, of course, and they are commonly encountered in sociology and many other fields. However, the most common type of survey is connected somehow with 'marketing research' or with 'opinion research'. Incidentally, the term 'market research' is generally brought into it somehow, although there used to be a clear distinction between that and marketing research. However, this isn't important to us here.

Marketing research, as such, is divided into various activities (industrial research, consumer research, product research, motivational research, sales research and media research). Opinion research (or 'polling') is intended to discover what the public think about issues and events. Marketing research (MR) is different because it sets out to find out about past behaviour, and therefore, assess future behaviour. Because opinion research has had some thoroughly publicised mistakes (election results ,usually) people tend to link MR with it and condemn it in the same way. But opinions can be deliberately falsified in some way: statements about behaviour are less easy to falsify.

So, how should you carry out the survey?
You have various possibilities:

1. Personal interviews
This depends upon two elements: the interviewer and the list of questions to be asked. Both have to be good. The interview may be taking place in public places (railway stations?), in homes, on doorsteps, and at places of work. The person being interviewed (respondent) is approached by the interviewer. This method is costly because of the need to pay for time (the right type of respondent is needed). Travelling expenses and experienced and

highly-trained interviewers have to be paid.

But the interviewer must not be prejudiced.

2. Group interview
This method is cheaper than some. We invite a cross-section of the population to be studied into the same room to discuss the subject in hand. A trained discussion leader (usually a psychologist) is in charge and the proceedings are normally recorded on tape.

This doesn't normally give rise to statistics but generalised broad views.

3. Postal questionnaires
This is expensive because you're lucky if you get 10% of the questionnaires back, completed properly! So we get a 'low response'. Postage and printing have to be paid for as well, but its the waiting that costs: awaiting the return, reminding potential respondents, waiting once more. The art is in constructing questions that are easy to answer ('yes' or 'no' replies are best). All effort asked for on the part of the respondent has to be limited.

4. Telephone surveys
Obviously these are restricted to people who have a telephone, and these people are not 'representative' of a wider population. The problem is that telephone calls can irritate potential respondents and one can't be sure they will be available when you ring.

5. Consumer panels
This will usually consist of some 2,000 persons (from whatever population is being considered). Each person is given a document for recording purchases, say, on a weekly basis (with whatever details are sought). These records are examined on a regular basis so that trends in purchasing can be determined, and so on.

6. Observation
In this case we simply count the number of something in a group (e.g. parked cars).

How is a survey set-up?
The Chart gives you an idea of the usual way to go about establishing the survey, and now we discuss the headings:

1. Establish the objective
Your key question is:

what decision will the survey assist?

Do avoid carrying out a survey 'in case we need the facts sometime'! This is because the 'facts' may be quickly out-of-date and will simply collect dust particles. Just as strange is the undertaking of a survey to back up a decision already taken!

2. Decide the type of presentation
If you decide about this now it will save time and data can be examined as it comes in. So you want to know how data are to be recorded on an 'ongoing' basis, and also how you'll finally present the information from your survey.

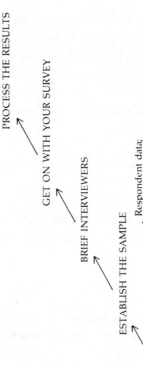

SETTING-UP YOUR SURVEY

PROCESS THE RESULTS

GET ON WITH YOUR SURVEY

BRIEF INTERVIEWERS

ESTABLISH THE SAMPLE

Respondent data;

DESIGN THE QUESTIONNAIRE – – Questions; dichotomous
open-ended
multiple

DECIDE THE TYPE OF PRESENTATION – – – for recording data; for the final presentation of the results.

ESTABLISH THE OBJECTIVE – – – What decisions will be taken as a result?

You're really looking at the kind of tables you want: you can always decide about supplementing this with barcharts and so on later on.

3. Design your questionnaire
Warning: this looks easy, but isn't!

You have to follow certain principles in framing your questiohs:
a. Questions must be devised so that they are
    ● instantly understood by the respondent;
    ● not in the least emotive;
    ● as impersonal as possible;
    ● actually capable of giving you the information you want!
b. The type of questions you can choose from are:
    ● 'dichotomous' (yes or no answers needed);
    ● 'open-ended' (the respondents own words give the answer); and
    ● 'multiple' (one answer chosen by the respondent from a selection).
    Of this collection, the 'open-ended' versions are the most difficult to cope with for *you* because the answer will be hard to categorise and slot into convienient groups for analysis. Questions beginning with 'Why did you?' may not be answered honestly anyway.
c. There will also have to be a survey identification on the questionnaire so that the form can be identified.

Respondent data (e.g. sex, age group) may be needed, but

'Questions should not be emotive'

do avoid asking too many personal questions. 'What age are you?' may appear rude, and ,anyway,you may get a lie!

4. *Establish the sample*
Even though you've produced the most exquistite questionnaire ever, it's still not able to be used. First of all, you have to decide whether you can use the questionnaire for the whole 'population' or only a "sample" of them. The former is the complete group (e.g. all the members of typing-pool, or all residents in a street), whereas the latter is a representative number of them taken from the former.

If you decide to use a sample, then be careful how you do it. We haven't the space here to discuss sampling fully, and you are recommended to use one of the excellent books suggested in the book-list to become better acquainted withe the procedure. Suffice it to say that you can get a *random* sample of, say the streets in a town and then get a random sample of the people living in those streets. The interviewer could be instructed to present his questionnaire to, say, the fiftieth person he or she meets, until 20 people have been approached. There are many ways of doing this.

5. *Brief interviewers*
Anyone who is going to go anywhere with your questionnaire could easily totally destroy the survey by doing it all wrong! Sometimes an interviewer may ask a question in such a tone that the respondent gets a hint of the expected 'right' answer! The briefing must emphasise

the need for neutrality on the part of the interviewer, and what has to be done in all possible eventualities.

6. *Getting on with the survey*

You may, if the survey is large and important to you, probably need to find out any snags beforehand. In which case you can go and do a small, experimental pilot (or prototype') survey to see what happens. This is a good way of testing your questionnaire, and making changes in the light of the experience gained.

7. *Processing results*

This may well be done partly while the survey is being undertaken i.e., as the forms come in. In any case, you will have to

- check the number of the forms returned;
- check their completeness;
- edit for mistakes and inconsistencies;
- classify and analyse any open-ended questions (or rather the answers!); and
- analyse the information you have now got.

What will be the result of all this?

If it's carried out as it should be, following the outline we've looked at above, then you will have the facts you want. But don't forget you have to find out *what* it is, exactly, you are looking for — or you shouldn't be surprised if you never get it!

When sampling is going to be involved, do take the trouble to find out about it, because some strange facts emerge, the results of a random sample survey will usually be more accurate than a total poplulation survey, and a fairly small sample will often do.

11. What do you know about percentages & ratios?

WHY BOTHER?

Largely because, as we have said before, absolute statistics (especially large numbers) haven't much impact when presented in a large lump.

Take the example of LS-S Company's past experience. The sales data may very well produce a rising line of trend on a chart. Good, so the firm is doing well, then! Well? No. Why? Because the profit isn't doing well. Suppose we see this from other statistics. Here we have, suddenly, a totally different, contradictory aspect. Yet......sales and profits aren't similar statistics, so how can we get some form of comparison?

Well, at least they are both measured in money terms. And isn't one linked (correlated?) to the other..... sales rise and so profits rise? In normal conditions, yes.

We might also be faced with the need to make some comparison between two sets of figures which don't have any known correlation. Or we may want to try and establish a correlation. In such a case, percentages would be useful because we could use this idea as a way of transforming the figures into a common dimension. We relate values, quantities, within each set of figures as percentages of the set's total and compare the two percentage lists.

It is also true that practically everybody accepts and knows about percentages. But often percentages conceal the important points about figures. For instance, if a geographical region shows that unemployed persons expressed as a % of total regional population is actually 10% whereas in all other regions the figure is 12%, then that's no great comfort, it is? Not, at least, to the region's residents. However, to Central Government, the percentages may well help to decide upon the allocation of aid.

Very often, the actual provision — the calculation — of percentage figures will have the important by product of giving rise to vital questions. So, regular statistics of this kind always generate an awareness of the need to monitor an organisation's progress.

But you have to be aware of little difficulties implied by percentages. Suppose your salary is cut by 10% in the next year. It is then increased by 10% for the following year. Are you now restored to your original salary? NO, you're not.

What we're saying here is that knowing what percentage means doesn't always suggest that we fully comprehend its uses and its significance! A safe rule is: only use a percentage in connection with other statistics if possible.

If you're going to insert % into your table, say, then also show what total 100% represents. Sceptics can then get out their calculators and work out the other absolute figures for themselves if the wish!

RATIOS? PROPORTIONS?

Actually, proportions and ratios are represented *by* percentages. As a rule, we'd adopt proportions as that they can be used in further ways.

In arithmetic terms, there is no difference at all between

$$\frac{7}{10} \quad \text{and} \quad \frac{70}{100}$$

or we could say '7 out of 10' instead.

Generally, what applies to percentages also applies to ratios and proportions.

PERCENTAGES AND STATISTICAL ANALYSIS

In the last Chapter we looked at surveys. Suppose, as a result of such a survey, concerning a new brand of soap we know that the market shares are:

First Quarter	Second Quarter
6.3%	9.3%

On the face of it, the soap appears to be selling well. The market (%) share is rising, but who is purchasing the soap? People who never buy it again? Who simply bought it just once? If this is the case, then sales are going to have to fall because the product's reputation ('Awful, don't buy it!') becomes known at large.

But if our survey was well constructed, it can deal with this information, too. We might have the following data:

First Quarter	Second Quarter
	New buyers: 7.0%
6.3%	
	Repurchasers: 2.3%

Now the position is clearer. Apparently if we calculate

$$(\frac{2.3}{6.3} \times 100) = 36.5$$

then we know that 36.5% of the new purchasers may also be future buyers (though we don't know for how long, do we?). This, by the way, in marketing, is a 'repeat-ratio' expressed as .37.

Given that this is true, then 36.5% of the new share in the Second Quarter would go over to the Third Quarter, and so forth. Needless to point out, other measures would also have to support this contention, but it is typical of a statistical idea emerging from survey information.

Just watch out how you use % and ratios!

12. Summary

The summary below highlights the vital steps in using statistics.

1. SET OBJECTIVES

What's the point, the motive, the purpose?
Who will see or use the results of our statistical effort?
To whom will *we* have to explain and perhaps justify what we have done?

2. COLLECT FIGURES

From where? Internally? Externally? Direct? How?
In what form? Units? Definitions?

3. PRESENT DATA, EXAMINE DATA

In what form? Reduced form?
How can the presentation assist examination of data?

4. ANALYSE CRITICALY

Trends? Seasons? Any quirks/peculiarities?
Comparisons?

5. INTERPRET YOUR DATA

Effects?
Suggestions?

6. FORECAST (where necessary)

How and why?

There are very few business problems indeed which cannot be assisted towards a solution by statistical treatment. Statistics, treated properly, will help to eliminate subjectivity and will help you to become more objective.

Don't forget cost-effectiveness, either. If a very simple, straightforward method will do, use it!

Reading list

ASHFORD, John
Statistics for management
2nd edition
London, Insitute of Personnel Management, 1980
458pp.

AUCHAMP, Johan (Editor)
The effective use of market research
London, Staples Press, 1071
320pp.

BARTHOLOMEW, David J. & FORBES, Andrew F.
Statistical techniques for manpower planning
Chichester, John Wiley, 1979
288pp.

BOOK, Stephen A.
Essentials of statistics
New York, McGraw-Hill, 1978
315pp.

BROCKINGTON, Raymond
Statistics for accountants and administrators
2nd edition
London, Gee & Co., 1974
176pp.

BRODIE, Morris
On thinking statistically: a short introduction
2nd edition
London, Heinemann, 1972
91pp.

CROFT, David
Applied statistics for management studies
2nd edition
London, Mcdonald and Evans, 1976
290pp.

FINANCIAL TIMES
Guide to FT statistics
London, 1973
32pp.

GREENSTED, C.S. & others
Essentials of statistics in marketing
London, Heinemann, 1974
257pp.

HARPER, W.M.
Statistics, 3rd edition
Plymouth, MacDonald and Evans Ltd., 1977
345pp.

HEDDERWICK Karl
Statistics for bargainers
London, Arrow Books, 1975
96pp.

HOLMAN, Leonard J.
Basic statistics for personnel managers
2nd edition
London, Institute of Personnel Management, 1979
66pp.

HUFF, Darrell
How to lie with statistics
London, Penguin, 1974
124pp.

ILERSIC, A.R. & PLUCK, R.A.
Statistics
14th edition
London, HFL., 1980

JOLLIFEE, F.R.
Commonsense statistics for economists and others
London, Routledge and Kegan Paul, 1974
174pp.

KENDALL, Maurice G. & BUCKLAND, William R.
A directory of statistical terms
3rd edition
Edinburgh, Oliver and Boyd 1971
166pp.

REICHARD, Robert S.
The numbers game: uses and abuses of managerial statistics
New York, McGraw-Hill, 1972
366pp.

WORCESTER, Robert W. (Editor)
Consumer market research handbook
London, McGraw-Hill, 1972
686pp.

Index

Other titles in the Management Update Checklist & Guide Series:

MAKING EFFECTIVE USE OF EXECUTIVE TIME by Bruce Austin
ISBN 0 946679 06 1 (Paperback)

MAKING YOUR MEETINGS MORE EFFECTIVE By Leonard Seymour-Smith
ISBN 0 946679 09 6 (Paperback)
     0 946679 10 X (Hardback)

Other Management Update titles

GETTING YOUR NEXT JOB: A guide to getting and succeeding at interviews by John Hallett
ISBN 0 946679 05 3 (Paperback)
     0 946679 07 X (Hardback)

UNDERSTANDING YOUR PENSION SCHEME: A guide to occupational pensions by David Hancox & Philip McMahon
ISBN 0 946679 03 7 (Paperback)
     0 946679 04 5 (Hardback)

REPORT WRITING: A practical guide to effective report writing presented in report form by Gordon Wainwright
ISBN 0 946679 01 0 (Paperback)
     0 946679 02 9 (Hardback)